Let Not Your Heart Be Troubled

John Fourteen:
Chapter of Resurrection Life

Robert C. McQuilkin

Columbia International University

Columbia, South Carolina

Let Not Your Heart Be Troubled / John Fourteen: Chapter of Resurrection Life

Copyright © 1941, 2012 by Columbia International University

7435 Monticello Rd.
Columbia, SC 29203
www.ciu.edu

Columbia International University exists to train men and women from a biblical world view to impact the nations with the message of Christ through service in the marketplace, missions and the local church.

Cover and interior book design by Kelly Smith, Tallgrass Media.
Cover photo by Augusto Avila Jr. (www.mediaskystudio.com)

First Printing: 1941

ISBN-13: 978-1-939074-00-3

Contents

Introduction to the Series

Dr. Robert C. McQuilkin served as the first president of Columbia International University, then named Columbia Bible College (CBC) for 29 years; 1923-1952. He served Christ and the Church as a magazine editor, dynamic speaker, and a prolific writer. But he also had a deep passion to teach. During his tenure as president, he taught Romans, John, Daniel and Revelation, Progress of Doctrine, Hermeneutics and other courses. The books in this series spilled over from those courses and from popular sermons he preached across the nation.

Dr. McQuilkin expressed the vision for a biblical university that outlines my own service as president: "Neither a Bible institute nor a liberal arts college, Columbia Bible College offers a curriculum with the spiritual advantages of the former, and the cultural advantages of the latter."

After Dr. McQuilkin's sudden death, G. Allen Fleece led the school in its move to CIU's present location. His plans for expansion laid the foundation for Dr. McQuilkin's son, Robertson who would become president in 1968 when Dr. Fleece returned to his first love of evangelism.

Robertson McQuilkin left the church planting work he loved in Japan to lead CIU from 1968 to 1990. Robertson, like his dad, writes, preaches, and teaches. His books on hermeneutics, world evangelization, ethics, and the Holy Spirit continue in print and are used by schools and ministries around the world.

On the occasion of CIU's 90th anniversary, join us in revisiting our rich heritage of the written works of Robert and Robertson McQuilkin. After all, together they provided leadership to CIU for over 50 years.

Within their writings, you will notice themes that form CIU's core values:

- Biblical Authority: The authority of Scripture as the defining rule for belief and practice.
- Victorious Christian Life: The victory in Christ that every Christian can experience through the filling of the Spirit.
- Prayer and Faith: The consistent practice by every Christian of personal witness to God's saving work in Christ.
- World Evangelization: The alignment of every Christian with God's heart for those around the world who have never heard the gospel.
- Evangelical Unity: Protecting the core truths of the faith, while seeking evangelical unity on all nonessentials.

We still live by these five core values as a school and to revisit them again in these books solidifies our commitment to them. We look back to remember and to underscore the importance of remaining tethered to our foundations, while exercising relevance in a dynamic, global community.

We look forward, until Christ returns, to serving His church by educating people from a biblical worldview to impact the nations with the message of Christ.

Dr. Bill Jones
President, Columbia International University
August 2012

Foreword

Why re-publish the writings of one who died more than a half century ago? Well, some would say, because they are classics by a major Christian author. But there's more.

Ninety years after their founding, very few institutions accurately reflect all the core values the founder held. But the grace of God through the creative genius of my father, Robert C. McQuilkin, has done just that. He was involved with initiating many movements and institutions. Some have morphed into something different than he envisioned. Some have disappeared. But the institution he poured his life into—Columbia Bible College—continues to this day in the vision and path he laid down, known today as Columbia International University.

Perhaps the enduring impact of his writing results in part, not only for its biblical fidelity on the God-intended life, but because his writing was signed and sealed by the life of the author. As I testified at his memorial service in 1952, "I know my father has sinned because 'all have sinned.' But I want you to know that for 25 years living in his house, I've never known him to fail."

At this celebration of God's faithfulness to Columbia International University, on its ninetieth birthday, how fitting that this treasure trove should once again be made available to the CIU family and, as in the beginning, far beyond.

J. Robertson McQuilkin
President Emeritus, Columbia International University
August 2012

Photo of Robertson McQuilkin with his father in the 1950s.

Outline of the Gospel of John

Text of John Fourteen

New King James Version (NKJV)

[1] "Let not your heart be troubled; you believe in God, believe also in Me. [2] In My Father's house are many mansions; if it were not so, I would have told you. I go to prepare a place for you. [3] And if I go and prepare a place for you, I will come again and receive you to Myself; that where I am, there you may be also. [4] And where I go you know, and the way you know."

[5] Thomas said to Him, "Lord, we do not know where You are going, and how can we know the way?"

[6] Jesus said to him, "I am the way, the truth, and the life. No one comes to the Father except through Me.

[7] "If you had known Me, you would have known My Father also; and from now on you know Him and have seen Him."

[8] Philip said to Him, "Lord, show us the Father, and it is sufficient for us."

[9] Jesus said to him, "Have I been with you so long, and yet you have not known Me, Philip? He who has seen Me has seen the Father; so how can you say, 'Show us the Father'? [10] Do you not believe that I am in the Father, and the Father in Me? The words that I speak to you I do not speak on My own authority; but the Father who dwells in Me does the works. [11] Believe Me that I am in the Father and the Father in Me, or else believe Me for the sake of the works themselves.

[12] "Most assuredly, I say to you, he who believes in Me, the works that I do he will do also; and greater works than these he will do, because I go to My Father. [13] And whatever you ask in My name, that I will do, that the Father may be glorified in the Son. [14] If you ask anything in My name, I will do it.

[15] "If you love Me, keep My commandments. [16] And I will pray the

Father, and He will give you another Helper, that He may abide with you forever— ¹⁷ the Spirit of truth, whom the world cannot receive, because it neither sees Him nor knows Him; but you know Him, for He dwells with you and will be in you. ¹⁸ I will not leave you orphans; I will come to you.

¹⁹ "A little while longer and the world will see Me no more, but you will see Me. Because I live, you will live also. ²⁰ At that day you will know that I am in My Father, and you in Me, and I in you. ²¹ He who has My commandments and keeps them, it is he who loves Me. And he who loves Me will be loved by My Father, and I will love him and manifest Myself to him."

²² Judas (not Iscariot) said to Him, "Lord, how is it that You will manifest Yourself to us, and not to the world?"

²³ Jesus answered and said to him, "If anyone loves Me, he will keep My word; and My Father will love him, and We will come to him and make Our home with him. ²⁴ He who does not love Me does not keep My words; and the word which you hear is not Mine but the Father's who sent Me.

²⁵ "These things I have spoken to you while being present with you. ²⁶ But the Helper, the Holy Spirit, whom the Father will send in My name, He will teach you all things, and bring to your remembrance all things that I said to you. ²⁷ Peace I leave with you, My peace I give to you; not as the world gives do I give to you. Let not your heart be troubled, neither let it be afraid. ²⁸ You have heard Me say to you, 'I am going away and coming back to you.' If you loved Me, you would rejoice because I said, 'I am going to the Father,' for My Father is greater than I.

²⁹ "And now I have told you before it comes, that when it does come to pass, you may believe. ³⁰ I will no longer talk much with you, for the ruler of this world is coming, and he has nothing in Me. ³¹ But that the world may know that I love the Father, and as the Father gave Me commandment, so I do. Arise, let us go from here.

Chapter 1

The Chapter of the Resurrection Life

Why has John Fourteen so gripped the hearts of Christians—high and low, rich and poor, schooled and unschooled? One reason is found in the opening sentence: "Let not your heart be troubled." All of the chapter is a setting forth of truth that is the secret of an untroubled heart. The command is repeated in verse twenty-seven: "Let not your heart be troubled, neither let it be afraid." A heart free from all anxiety and from all fear—that is the longing of every human being.

John Fourteen is the best-loved chapter of the New Testament, as the Twenty-third Psalm is the best-loved chapter of the Old.

The disciple whom Jesus loved wrote the Gospel that all Christians love. The Gospel according to John is the book of "Christ our Life." The fourteenth chapter of John is a chapter of resurrection life; and the Twenty-third Psalm is the Psalm of resurrection life.

Nearly all Christians can repeat from memory the Twenty-third Psalm. Not many could repeat the thirty-one verses of John Fourteen, nor tell with any completeness what the message of the chapter is.

This farewell message of the Lord Jesus is in the nature of His last will and testament to His loved ones who were to be left in the world. And what an inheritance it was! He was leaving them peace—"perfect peace in this dark world of sin." He was leaving them life—eternal life. The cost of this treasure He was bequeathing was His own death: "For where there is a testament, there must also of necessity be the death of the testator. For a testament is in force after men are dead, since it has no power at all while the testator lives." (Heb. 9:16, 17). Because He lived after death, we also shall live (14:19).

Let us examine this inheritance as set forth in John Fourteen. For all the wealth of the riches of a billionaire cannot be compared to the wealth of the man who possesses the riches of John Fourteen. Yet these riches belong to the humblest child of God. Are we making use of them? The first step is to know what they are, in order that we may lay hold of them in the way that is clearly set forth.

Christ came that we might have life, that we might have life abundantly. This is resurrection life, the abundant life, a victorious life, the Christ-controlled life, the Spirit-filled life, the life of peace and joy and power. This is the life for which Christians long. John Fourteen is a revelation of life from Him who is the Life.

THE GEM IN ITS SETTING

What is the setting of John Fourteen in the book of John, and in the whole Bible?

John fourteen to sixteen has been called the holy place of the Bible, and John seventeen, the holy of holies. The fourth Gospel itself is the central book of the Bible. It is the spiritual interpreter of the first three Gospels. It looks back toward all that has gone before, beginning in eternity, and it points forward to the new dispensation of the Spirit.

John tells us clearly his purpose in writing the Gospel: "but these are written that you may believe that Jesus is the Christ, the Son of God, and that believing you may have life in His name." (20:31). In these words we might state also the purpose of each of the other Gospels and the purpose of the whole Bible.

The witness of John the Baptist to the Lord Jesus as recorded in the Gospel of John included two great revelations as to who Jesus was, and two great revelations as to what Jesus was to do. He was the Christ, or the Messiah, and He was the Son of God. He came to do two things: He came to die for the sin of the world, as the Lamb of God; and He came to baptize in the Holy Spirit. All the events in the Gospel moved toward that great consummation of the coming of the Holy Spirit, made possible only when Christ was glorified through death and resurrection.

Dr. W. J. Erdman, and probably others, have seen in John 16:28 a striking summing up of the message of the Gospel, in the order of its presentation: "I came forth from the Father, and have come into the world: again, I leave the world, and go to the Father."

First of the four sections of the Gospel is the sublime preview in the first eighteen verses: "I came forth from the Father.

There follows the revelation to the world in John 1:19 to 12:50, "and I have come into the world."

When the moment came for Him to leave the world, there came the moment for the revelation to the inner circle. In the twelfth chapter we are told that He hid Himself from the world, and from chapter thirteen to seventeen He gives His marvelous revelation to the inner circle, telling His own the things they need to know because He is leaving the world, "Again, I leave the world."

In the closing chapters, we have the glorification of Christ in death and resurrection, "And go to the Father."

The fourteenth chapter has a special place in this revelation to the inner circle. It was the portion of the message spoken in the upper room probably before they left the room and went toward the Garden of Gethsemane. The chapter closes, "Arise, let us go from here."

There is needed a preparation of heart to hear the message of John Fourteen. The disciples who first listened to the precious words needed to have prepared hearts. The thirteenth chapter tells how our Lord prepared them.

For one thing, Judas must be separated from the company. He did not belong to the inner circle. "You are clean, but not all," our Lord told them.

The disciples who were left after Judas went out into everlasting darkness were true believers. They were vitally joined to Christ; but they were defeated disciples. Their hearts were not prepared to receive this farewell message. On the way to the upper room they had been disputing as to who should be greatest. To them this was a very practical question. Our Lord had predicted His death, but they did not hear this part of His prophecy. He had also said that they would sit on twelve thrones, judging the twelve tribes of Israel. They did hear this, and their thought was that He would set up His kingdom when they entered Jerusalem. This is why John and James had come to ask for the chief places at the right hand and at the left hand of Christ.

With proud hearts, then, the disciples came to the upper room. The Lord Jesus was on the way to the cross. He knew that all things had been given into His hand. He knew that He came from God and was going to God. Knowing all these things, knowing that He was God, He was on the way to take the place of utmost humiliation and of lowest shame. The mind of Christ was this mind of uttermost humility. The mind of the disciples was the mind of pride.

It seems evident that when they reached the upper room, there was a moment of embarrassment; the question must have risen in their minds as to who should wash the feet of the guests before they were seated. John, as the youngest, was the natural one to do it. But how would it look for one who aspired to sit at the right hand of the King to take the place of a servant? Judas certainly would not do it. Peter, as the leader of the twelve, could not think of doing it. So they seated themselves with unwashed feet, and with uncleansed hearts.

Here, as always in the presence of Christ, "Where sin abounded, grace abounded much more." Our Lord used this situation to give to them and to us one of His most precious messages. The Lord Himself washed their feet. It was no outward ceremony; the feet needed cleansing; the water and the towel had gone unused. From this washing of the disciples' feet, our Lord gave two distinct teachings. The primary purpose of His action was to show them that they should do lowly service one for the other. They were to have the mind of Christ, expressed in lowly service. He was on the way to the cross, taking the lowest place that man could take in His love for them and for all men. As He was in their midst as one who serves, so should they be.

When Peter refused to have his feet washed, the Lord took occasion to give another spiritual teaching: "If I do not wash you, you have no part with Me." Impetuous Peter then rushed from his declaration that Jesus should never wash his feet to the other extreme: "Lord, not my feet only, but also my hands and my head." But the disciples were bathed, and it was only the feet that had accumulated the dust by the wayside that needed cleansing. So our Lord told them they were clean, with the exception of Judas, clean in their right attitude toward Him as Saviour and Lord; yet they needed His daily cleansing. He did not mean that Christians were to cleanse one another's feet in the sense of forgiving them their sins; He only can do that. We are to have the attitude of loving, lowly service, even as He. This is taking up His cross and following Him.

The thirteenth chapter, saddened by the prophecy that one of the disciples was to betray Him, closes with another sad revelation that Peter, the leader of the twelve, would deny Him. The time is drawing nigh to midnight, on Thursday, the day before He went to the cross. It is at that dark moment the gracious words fall from His lips: "Let not your heart be troubled."

Is your heart disturbed, or puzzled, or saddened, or harassed by cares, or by fears? Our Lord covers all of these sicknesses of mind and heart in His word, "Let not your heart be troubled."

TEN THREES OF JOHN FOURTEEN

Like First John, and like the seventeenth chapter of John, the fourteenth chapter defies analysis or outlining; perhaps we might better say, transcends any outline. Like other portions of the inspired Word, it may be studied from many viewpoints. As from the facets of a diamond there shine out glorious rays of light that reveal the beauty of the precious gem, so with this perfect diamond of eternal truth.

For the study of great doctrines of the Christian faith, there is a wealth of material in John Fourteen. Consider how clear and blessed is the teaching on these doctrines: the trinity, the deity of Christ, the Holy Spirit, heaven, eternal life, prayer, service, the second coming of Christ, death, resurrection, Satan, the world, faith, revelation, the indwelling of Christ.

But for our present meditation on the fourteenth chapter of John, we are not to take up these doctrines one by one, nor to give a commentary on each verse. We are to gather out several threefold messages imbedded in the chapter use them as searchlights on eternal treasures.

Before we meditate on these clusters of truth, the reader might like first to search the chapter and discover for himself that these things are there.

There are three Persons in John Fourteen: Father, Son, and Spirit. The chapter is one of the greatest revelations of Scripture concerning the trinity. There are three Disciples whom the Lord addresses, and these disciples ask three Questions. The English word "mansions" is mentioned only in John 14:2. But in the chapter there are three Mansions, or abiding places, mentioned. There are three Gifts and three Commands, and three Prayers. There are three Enemies, although only two are mentioned directly. There are three Comings of Christ set forth. And if we desire to complete a group of ten threes, we shall see that our threefold salvation, expressed in the three great words that sum up the Christian life—faith, hope, and love—is blessedly presented in John Fourteen, although not specifically referred to, as in the case of the other threes.

It would be helpful to search into the unsearchable riches of Christ by a method like this, even if there were no special significance in having three questions, or three commands, or three gifts. But it will be seen that these various threes present a complete view of some spiritual truth. Their messages intertwine, and press home again and again the same glorious facts. Yet there is a distinct message in each cluster, and their study should help Christians to understand the mighty mysteries of our union with God in Christ, and the great foundations on which our eternal life and our present victory rest.

Chapter 2

The Three Persons[1]

Our Lord's farewell revelation to the inner circle at the close of His earthly ministry is preeminently a revelation of Father, Son, and Holy Spirit. It is altogether fitting that when He was to leave the world and go to the Father's house, He should reveal to the disciples the relationship between the Father and Himself, and the new miracle that was to take place in the sending of God the Holy Spirit. The Gospel is presented in John as a revelation of the Father. The theme of John Fourteen might be stated thus: "Christ the only way to the Father: Relation of Father, Son and Holy Spirit."

John wrote his Gospel in order that men might believe that Jesus is the Christ, the Son of God. All through the book we have multiplied proofs that Jesus is God.

1. He is called God (1:1; 1:18).
2. Jews condemned Him for making Himself God (5:18; 10:30-33).
3. The title "Son of God" means He is God (5:18; 19:7).
4. He does what only God can do (1:3; 5:21-22).
5. He receives worship as God (5:23; 9:38; 20:28).
6. The attributes or perfections of God are ascribed to Him (1:1,2; 3:35; 16:15).
7. His own claims with reference to the Father (5:17; 10:30; 17).
8. His name is linked with the Father, as no man's could be (14:1; 17:3)

---

1 Some may prefer to postpone reading this chapter on the trinity and go first to the other "threes".

9. He is identified with Jehovah of the Old Testament (12:38-41).

10. He is supernatural in His pre-existence, birth, resurrection, ascension, present position (1:1; 3:13; 6:62; 16:28; 17:5).

When Philip said, "Lord, show us the Father," the answer had in it a gentle rebuke and a touch of disappointment: "Have I been with you so long, and yet you have not known Me, Philip? He who has seen Me has seen the Father; so how can you say, 'Show us the Father'?"

Everything He had been doing during His ministry was just that—to show them the Father: "I am in the Father, and the Father in me" (v. 11). Throughout the message our Lord Jesus speaks of Himself and of God the Father as no man could do: "You believe in God, believe also in Me." He speaks not of their keeping the commandments of God, but of keeping His commandments.

When the Lord Jesus speaks of "My Father," He is calling God "His own Father" (John 5:18). The Jews recognized that this meant that He was making Himself equal with God.

Christ presents Himself as doing what only God can do. It is He who is to prepare a place in heaven for His disciples. It is He who gives them His peace, which is the peace of God that passes all understanding.

The Holy Spirit is presented in John Fourteen as a person and as God. Our Lord speaks of Him as "another Comforter." The Greek word is "Paraclete" and means literally, "one called to be alongside of." The Holy Spirit is spoken of by our Lord always as a person. The world "beholds him not, neither sees Him nor knows Him; but you know Him, for He dwells with you and will be in you."

Every Christian doctrine goes beyond human reason, but never contradicts human reason. So it is with the doctrine of the trinity. Not only is the doctrine of three persons in the Godhead a reasonable doctrine, but no other teaching would be reasonable. God is love, and from all eternity before there were any created beings, God was (or rather is) complete in

Himself. He always had an object of love. There was the ineffable love of Father, Son, and Holy Spirit.

The wisest theologians who study the depths of this revelation of the trinity are face to face with mysteries that go beyond their reason. But the humblest Christian has no difficulty with the truth of the trinity in actual experience. As Father, Son, and Spirit are presented in their varied and beautiful relations in John Fourteen, so in the heart of the Christian, there is no difficulty in recognizing one God, and in recognizing that Father, Son, and Spirit are always joined together in everything that God is, and in everything that God accomplishes.

A further mystery is added because the Lord Jesus is man as well as God. The second person of the trinity, infinite God, became finite. He was incarnate as man. The Lord Jesus is perfect man, and fully man in every point, as well as fully God. In becoming finite, we do not mean that the Lord Jesus gave up His infinity. He did voluntarily limit Himself in the days of His flesh, so that He could speak of the Father's knowing things which the Son (in His human nature) did not know.

In all the work of creation, and in the work of salvation, or the new creation, Father, Son, and Spirit are joined together, but there is this order in their operation:

1. All things come from God the Father as the Source.
2. All things come through God the Son as the Channel.
3. All things come by God the Holy Spirit, as the Agent.

This wonderful operation of Father, Son, and Spirit is set forth in the gracious words of John Fourteen.

God in His essential eternal being is, and has been from all eternity, without beginning, Father, Son, and Spirit. These are not merely different names for the same Person, nor different manifestations of the one Person. If God had not become man, we never would know God directly. We would only know things concerning God which an angel might tell us. But this man sitting with these disciples on that Thursday night before He was lifted up on the cross, is in His own being the mighty God, speaking to men.

Some have been puzzled by our Lord's statement in John 14:28, "for my Father is greater than I." Our Lord, speaking not only in His humanity, but in His humility, could say that the Father was greater than He. But some judge that the sense in which He could use that term was in the sense of relationship: father is greater than son, even though father and son are equally human; so, the Father might be spoken of as greater than the Son, though both are equally divine.

While Father, Son, and Spirit are equal in power and glory, and are always associated in whatever God does, yet there is an order of operation, and there is an order of what the theologians call subsistence. The order is always Father, Son, and Spirit. When we speak of the sonship of the Lord Jesus, we must not think in terms of a human son who is begotten by his father and thus has a beginning later than his father. The sonship of Christ to the eternal Father does not refer to any beginning in time; it refers to relationship.

However, the real thought in the mind of the Lord must be found in the purpose of that statement, "My Father is greater than I." He is telling them that they ought to rejoice because He is going to the Father. He said that they were going to do greater works than the works that He had done, and the reason was, "Because I go to the Father." Who was to do these greater works? It was the risen Christ at the right hand of God. God the Father turned all of His authority and power over to the Son. At this moment the mighty power of God is exercised not by the Father, but by the Son. This in itself proves that the Son is God. Christ at the right hand of God now, has a power that He did not have here on earth. But one will say, He was God when He was on earth. Quite true. But He was the self-limited God, incarnate as man, and laying aside the use of His mighty power.

Yet there is a still deeper thought here. He was to be glorified in death and resurrection, and then the one who had gone to the place of utmost humility was to be raised to the place of fullness of power. It was the Father who gave Him this position and thus in one sense of the word, the Father is "greater." Thus we read that He that sends is greater than He that is sent. But all this is no contradiction of the other great truths that Jesus is God equal with the Father, though in these other senses the Father is greater than He.

Now that Christ has this power, we may truly say that the risen Christ is greater than the One who spoke to those disciples. And yet the One who stood before them was the mighty God incarnate in man.

Our intellect staggers at the greatness of these conceptions. But when we kneel down to pray, we have no difficulty in speaking to our Father in the name of the Lord Jesus, and never have any consciousness of addressing three Gods, nor any confusion in the thought of worshipping three Gods. Our hearts worship one God. Neither, on the other hand, is there any confusion in recognizing Father, Son, and Spirit.

With such a Father, and such a Saviour, and such a Comforter, should it be hard to obey His command, "Let not your heart be troubled"?

Chapter 3

The Three Disciples

We would know nothing of Thomas and Philip and Judas (not Iscariot), the three disciples mentioned in John Fourteen, apart from the Gospel of John. Nor would we know anything personally about Nathanael and Andrew. John is the personal Gospel, and it gives intimate glimpses into the souls of those disciples, of whom no details are given in the other Gospels.

We are particularly interested in the three questions asked by these three disciples. But before considering the questions, it will be helpful to get acquainted with the disciples.

THE FIRST DISCIPLE

When we think of Thomas we are likely to think of "Thomas, the doubter," but it would be better to remember his glorious outburst of faith, "My Lord and my God." In any case, his characteristic was not so much that of doubting as of wistful pessimism. Our first introduction to Thomas was when the Lord announced to the disciples that Lazarus was dead and that He was going to Bethany, near Jerusalem, to awaken him of sleep. Thomas said to his fellow disciples, "Let us also go, that we may die with him." Here two characteristics were suggested. One was a devoted loyalty to the Lord Jesus that would want to go and die with Him; the other was the attitude of expecting the worst to happen. The Lord on that trip was to go to raise Lazarus. Thomas, knowing how the Jews were seeking to kill Him, expected that He would be put to death.

When the disciples told Thomas that the Lord was risen and had appeared to them, this seemed to him to be entirely too good to be true. His remark, as recorded in the fourteenth chapter of John, was also in keeping with this characteristic of a loyal, devoted, but wistful, pessimistic character. What a transformation Christ made in one who was ever thinking that it was too good to be true, to expect the very best to happen!

THE SECOND DISCIPLE

Our first introduction to Philip is when the Lord Jesus personally finds Philip and says, "Follow me." Philip finds Nathanael, and says to him, "We have found him, of whom Moses in the Law and in the Prophets, wrote, Jesus of Nazareth, the son of Joseph." This suggests a practical turn of mind, dealing with the facts as they are, the things that one can see. At the feeding of the five thousand, the Lord tests Philip by asking, "Where shall we buy bread, that these may eat?" Philip calculates how much it would cost to buy bread for that multitude. This suggests a practical mind, and also a mind that does not easily turn in faith expecting a supernatural thing to be done. When the Greeks came to Philip to ask him about seeing Jesus, probably for a special personal interview, Philip came to Andrew first, and together they went to Jesus. When Philip said, "Lord, show us the Father," in John Fourteen, it was in keeping with his character; he wanted to have things proved to him so that he could see.

THE THIRD DISCIPLE

We know nothing of Judas, apart from his question recorded in John Fourteen. However, a comparison with the lists of disciples suggests that this Judas is identical with the one who is called Lebbaeus, whose surname was Thaddaeus, probably the brother of James the Less. The descriptive names given him mean "a beloved child." What a blessed contrast this suggests to Judas Iscariot. And in his question, he addresses Jesus as "Lord." It has been noted that Judas Iscariot is never quoted as calling Jesus "Lord."

It is quite possible that he did call him that, without really meaning it; no man can say "Jesus is Lord," except in the Holy Spirit. So Judas Iscariot never really called Jesus "Lord," but Judas (not Iscariot) loved the Lord Jesus, and it is very fitting that Christ's message to this "beloved child" should be a message concerning the Father's love.

We also are children of His love. When we know His personal interest in each individual disciple, need we have troubled hearts?

Chapter 4

The Three Questions

Throughout the heathen world, among the millions who have never heard of Christ, there are three questions concerning eternal things that occupy the hearts of men.

The first question is, "What is the way to heaven?"

There is no question that there is to be a future life, and there is no question about the fact that there is a heaven and a hell.

Missionaries laboring among primitive tribes in Africa have found that one of the names of God in the native language is this: "The one who blesses indiscriminately here, and who separates for blessing hereafter." All nations of men know, however vaguely, that there is future bliss and future torment. Hence the great question their religions attempt to answer is, "What is the way to heaven?"

The second question that these religions seek to answer is, "What is heaven like?" The religions give varied pictures of bliss in the future life, from the Buddhist Nirvana, the closest that human conception can get to nothingness, to a heaven of sensual delight as pictured for faithful Muslims.

If the human heart were satisfied as to the answer to these two questions, there would remain only one other question, "What about the time between now and that future bliss? What is the secret of joy and peace and happiness in the present life?"

In John Fourteen three disciples ask three questions. The Lord Jesus really drew out these questions from the disciples, and then gave answers of soul-satisfying certainty.

THE FIRST QUESTION

Jesus told the disciples that He was going away, and He told them that He was going to prepare a place for them in the Father's house. And then He said, "And where I go you know, and the way you know" (v. 4).

"Thomas said to Him, 'Lord, we do not know where You are going, and how can we know the way?' " (v. 5).

When Peter said, "Lord, where are You going?" and when Thomas said, "We do not know where You are going," they had in mind some earthly journey. They did not understand the meaning of His going to the Father's house. Sorrow filled their hearts because He said He was to leave them and they were not occupied with the wonder of the Father's house and what it would mean to them to have Him go.

But it was the Lord's desire to show them the way, and He answered Thomas' question in those marvelous words: "I am the way, the truth, and the life" (v. 6).

"What is the way to heaven?" The answer is Jesus.

The Greek words may be translated: "I am the way, both the truth and the life." This brings out the meaning of salvation. The Lord Jesus is the way to God. He is not the "way-show-er." He does not point men toward God, and leave them to follow on the way, and then come into the presence of God. The Lord Jesus is Himself the Way. When we get to Jesus, we are there, in the very presence of God.

Christ is the revelation of the truth. But to look at Him who is the truth, brings the realization that the truth condemns us. We have not done the truth. We are contrary to the truth. We are dead in trespasses and sins. If the law was a mirror let down from heaven in which men might see themselves and their undone condition, much more was the incarnate Son of God the perfect mirror of God in which we men might see our utterly undone condition. But He is also the Life. Only one who can give life can bring salvation to lost men whom the truth condemns.

If the law "could have given life, truly righteousness would have been by the law" (Galatians 3:21). But the law could not give life. Christ is the life. "Jesus is the way, both the truth and the life."

But that was not all the Lord said in answering the question. He added, "No one comes to the Father except through Me." He is not only the all-sufficient way to heaven, He is the only way. There is no other. As one has said, "There may be comparative religions, but Christianity is not one of them." The Christian faith is never called a religion in the Bible. It was called "the Faith" and also "the Way." Christianity is Christ, and Christ is the way.

How solemn is this word, that none can come to God except through Jesus, and how loosely men deal with it today. They suppose that the Jews have denied the Lord Jesus but that they worship God the Father. If this were so, then the word of Jesus is not a true word. When the Jews deny the Son, they deny the Father. God may in His mercy answer an unsaved man's prayer in order that the goodness of God may lead him to repentance. But He does not guarantee to answer any man's prayer except it be in the name of Christ.

As surely as Jesus is the way, the truth, and the life, so surely there is no other way to the Father.

Multitudes today are asking why we should take "Christianity" to the heathen nations when they have religions of their own. Why should we seek to have a man change his religion? The answer is that missionaries do not go to have men change their religions. They go to give them Christ, who alone is their Life. They go to tell them the answer to the questions of their own hearts, "What is the way to heaven? What is the way to God?"

THE SECOND QUESTION

As the Lord continued His discourse, He drew out the next question: "If you had known Me, you would have known My Father also; and from now on you know Him and have seen Him" (v. 7). All through His ministry, the Lord Jesus had been making a revelation of the Father. He was longing that the disciples should understand the revelation. Philip probably expressed the thought of the other disciples when he said, "Lord, show us the Father, and it is sufficient for us" (v. 8).

Philip spoke truly when he said that to see the Father would satisfy the human heart. Nothing else will satisfy the human heart. But if there is a way to show us the Father, that is enough. That was our Lord's purpose in all His association with these men. So He answered, "Have I been with you so long, yet you have not known Me, Philip?" (v. 9). The thought is, "Do you not recognize who I am?"

The answer to the question, "What is heaven like?" is that heaven is the Father's house. When our Lord said, "In my Father's house are many mansions," He said more about heaven in a single sentence than volumes of man's speculation might reveal. Heaven is the Father's house. If we know what God is like, we shall know what kind of a place heaven is. Of course, heaven is an entirely satisfying place, because God the Father completely satisfies the human heart.

The answer to the question, "What is God like?" is, "He is like Jesus." And so our Lord said to Philip: "He who has seen Me has seen the Father; so how can you say, 'Show us the Father?'" (v. 9)

Some people wonder whether there will be enough in heaven to interest them. Is God enough? If we think of the greatest joy, and bliss, and pleasure, and beauty, and knowledge, and triumph, and love, and power, and service possible to men on earth, and multiply that by infinity and stretch it out to eternity, we have a little glimpse of what heaven will be.

THE THIRD QUESTION

But there remains the third question, "What about the present life?" No man can be truly happy unless he is absolutely assured that he is saved and on the way to heaven, and unless he is assured that heaven will completely satisfy him. With those two questions settled, there remains only the question as to the time between now and when we reach the Father's house. This question is gloriously answered when one of the disciples asked the Lord something, which does not seem directly related to it: "Judas (not Iscariot) said to Him, 'Lord, how is it that You will manifest Yourself to us, and not to the world?'"(v.22)

These Jewish disciples naturally were looking forward to the time when Messiah would be manifested to all the world, and all men would bow before Him. They did not understand as yet the place of this present dispensation, when the Lord Jesus would be at the right hand of God and they would be witnessing unto Him until that great day when Christ should return again. The Lord answered the question, as always, by going to the heart of the practical message: "If anyone loves me, he will keep My words: and My Father will love him and We will come to him, and make our home with him" (v. 23).

This means that during the time when Christ is in heaven preparing a place for His disciples, the Father and the Son (and also the Holy Spirit, as is made clear to them a moment later) will come and abide in their hearts. In other words, they will have a foretaste of heaven on earth. The earnest of the Spirit is an experience now of the glories that will be ours completely when redemption is finished. The time has not yet come for Christ to be manifested to the world, but the time is present when He is manifested to those who believe in Him, and who are loved of the Father. Could anything be more sublime? The mighty God, the triune God, Father, Son, and Holy Spirit, taking up His abode in the human heart—truly, this is a greater miracle than the physical birth of the Son of God in the womb of the Virgin Mary.

The answer to every question is "Jesus," and we have Him. With all questions answered we may indeed have untroubled hearts.

Chapter 5

The Three Mansions

The word "mansions" occurs only once in the Bible, in John 14:2, "In my Father's house are many mansions." The Greek word that is translated "mansions," occurs only twice in the Bible, in John 14:2 and in John 14:23.

The word means "abiding places". Of course, these abiding places are but faintly foreshadowed by the most beautiful mansions ever designed by gifted architects.

THE FIRST MANSION

When the Lord told the disciples that there were many abiding places in his Father's house, He added the significant word, "If it were not so, I would have told you." The Lord never hesitated to tell the disciples truth that would be disappointing to them. He never failed to clear up their false conception of spiritual things. There is a hint here that the truth about spiritual things is far greater than anything we realize. If it were less than we imagine, then the Lord would have told us. He makes it still stronger by adding, "I go to prepare a place for you." Beautiful mansions do not just happen. They need careful and long preparation. What shall we say about the places that Christ is preparing? He has been there at the Father's right hand for nineteen hundred years, and all of His activities have a bearing on the preparing of a place for believers.

There are many abiding places. That is, there is abundant room for all believers. They are personally prepared places. As each of these eleven apostles was individually known and loved by the Lord, so is each individual believer known and loved by the Lord. If a good earthly father knows all of his children, and loves each of them with all his heart, will the Heavenly Father's love be less?

This is real "security." Before the [first] world war, the biggest question in the minds of many people was the question of "security"—social security, financial security, security for old age, security against unforeseen circumstances. The only secure abiding places are those that the Lord Jesus Christ is preparing in the Father's house. Perhaps Peter was thinking of that upper-room message when he wrote of "an inheritance incorruptible, and undefiled, and that does not fade away, reserved in heaven for you" (1 Pet. 1:4).

THE SECOND MANSION

The only other time that this word for mansion, or abiding place, is used is in our Lord's wonderful word in verse 23: "My Father will love him, and We will come to him, and make Our home with him."

What a revelation is here! While the Lord Jesus at the right hand of God is preparing a mansion for us in heaven, the Father, Son, and Holy Spirit come and take up their mansion in a human heart. Surely, that is heaven on earth. No wonder that the Holy Spirit is called an earnest of our future complete inheritance. One of these facts is as literally true as the other: He is really preparing a place for us; the Father and Son and Spirit really have taken up an abiding place in the hearts of believers.

Paul speaks of God's making known to the saints the riches of the glory of the great new mystery revealed in a special way through him, "which is Christ in you, the hope of glory" (Col 1:27). The indwelling Christ is the pledge of future glory, and a foretaste of future glory, which will be complete likeness to Christ. How Paul exulted in the truth, "Christ lives in me"!

We shall have further light upon this wonderful indwelling of Christ when we consider other threefold clusters of truth. It is clear, from this revelation, that when Christ lives in the human heart, the triune God is there. Father, Son, and Spirit are united in the great work of redemption, and the Father, Son, and Holy Spirit are abiding in the hearts of believers.

THE THIRD MANSION

There is a third mansion suggested in John Fourteen, although not directly mentioned. While the noun for "abiding place" occurs only twice, the verb is used many times. In John 15:4 we read, "Abide in me, and I in you." The third mansion or abiding place is the Lord Jesus Christ Himself. He is living in us. We are living in Him. This truth is included also in John Fourteen: "I am in my Father, and you in Me, and I in you" (v. 20).

Can we glimpse the wonder of the fact that all that is true of Christ as our Saviour belongs to us? We are in Him. Did He die on the cross and pay the eternal death penalty for sin? We are in Him, and when He died, we died. Did He rise again and conquer death? Did He ascend above all principalities and powers? Did He defeat Satan? He did it all for us. We are in Him. He is our abiding place. All that He has is ours. We are complete in Him, and the Christian life is briefly and wonderfully comprehended in these seven words, "Abide in me, and I in you," or in the seven words of John 14:20, "You in me, and I in you." The fifteenth chapter of John, and the chapters of First John, may be taken as a commentary on this great truth of our abiding place in Christ.

Do we ourselves have a responsibility with regard to these mansions? Will our Christian life now make a difference then? We recall the servant who invested his pound and made ten pounds; his lord made him ruler over ten cities. It does make a difference how we invest time and money and strength for the Lord here on earth. We are training here for our abiding places there.

"The angels from their thrones on high, Look down on us with wondering eye, That where we are but passing guests, We build

such strong and solid nests, But where we hope to dwell for aye,
We scarce take heed one stone to lay." [author unkown]

For troubled hearts, what rest and relaxation and comfort and riches could be compared with the provision in these three "mansions"?

Chapter 6

The Three Gifts

A human gift is usually measured by two things. One is the love that the giver has for the one who is to receive the gift. The other is the wealth of the giver. There is a third thing that should condition a gift, the power of the one who receives the gift to appreciate and to use it.

Every good gift and every perfect gift is from above and comes down from the Father (James 1:17). The measure of God's giving is the measure of God's love for His Son. There is unmeasured love. There is unmeasured power. There is unmeasured capacity to receive. And so we read: "For God does not give the Spirit by measure. The Father loves the Son, and has given all things into his hand." (John 3:34, 35). Our Lord also testified, "All things that the Father has are mine" (John 16:15).

THE FIRST GIFT

Now Christ is God's unspeakable gift to us. First, He gave His Son all things. Then He gave us Christ, and with Christ He freely gave us all things (Rom. 8:32). The gift of Christ Himself is one of the three gifts presented in John Fourteen. Christ is our life. The first gift is eternal life. That gift comes first to the lost sinner who takes Christ as his Saviour. We have already considered the teaching that Christ is the way to the Father, and He is the only way. He is "the life." In order that we might have that gift of life, Christ must die. This message is the farewell message before He goes to the cross. He says that the prince of the world comes, and then He says, "As the Father gave me commandment, even so I do. Arise, let us go from here." These words have a deeper meaning than rising and leaving the upper room. He is going straightforward to the cross. According to the commandment of His Father, He is laying down His life (John 10:17-18).

But Christ who laid down His life for us will also rise for us. He is the Father's Gift to the disciples, and "because I live, you shall live also" (v. 19).

THE SECOND GIFT

The Father has another gift for His children. One may ask how God can give anything more than His beloved Son. In one sense, He cannot give more than His beloved Son. And yet there must be a reason for another unspeakable gift of the Father and the Son. "And I will pray the Father, and He will give you another Helper, that He may abide with you forever—the Spirit of truth, whom the world cannot receive, because it neither sees nor knows Him; but you know Him; for he dwells with you, and will be in you" (vss. 16, 17).

The gift of the Holy Spirit may be thought of as the central theme of John fourteen, fifteen, and sixteen. He told the disciples that it was better for them that He should go away. The disciples' hearts were filled with sorrow because the Lord told them He was going away. Yet He said that it was expedient, or better, for them that He go away, "For if I do not go away, the Helper (Comforter) will not come to you; but if I depart, I will send Him unto you" (16:7).

Would we be willing to exchange our last month's experience of Christ, or our last year's experience, for such an experience as the disciples had when Jesus was with them in the flesh? Is it really true that we may today have a better experience of Christ than the disciples had? That is what He is saying to them. If He were telling them that another Comforter would come to take the place of Himself, they could scarcely rejoice in that. But He is telling them of the coming of One who would bring Christ Himself closer to them.

This coming One is "another Comforter." He is as definitely a Person as the Lord Jesus is. The word "Comforter" means much more than "consoler," or one who comforts in sorrow. He is to be the teacher. He is the strengthener. He is the miracle worker. He is to be to them all that Jesus was. Indeed, all that the Lord Jesus did in the days of His flesh He did by the power of the Holy Spirit. This same Holy Spirit was now to come into the disciples and make Christ real in and through them. How does He do it? He takes the things of Christ and makes them real to them.

We have noted that God gives to Christ everything. Then He gives us Christ, and with Christ He freely gives us all things. Then He sends the Holy Spirit, who takes the things of Jesus and makes them real to us.

We may study the earthly life of the Lord Jesus and learn what are the things He had. He had two great certainties in His life: He was sure of the Father, and He was sure of God's plan for His life. He had peace and joy. He was also the man of sorrows and acquainted with grief. He was a man of prayer. He was a man who lived in the Word of God. He took the right view toward money, and toward worldly things; He was utterly separated from the world. Above all things, He loved men; He came to seek and to save that which was lost.

How startling a thing it is that when the Holy Spirit came at Pentecost and filled these disciples, the qualities that were in the Lord Jesus were made real in their lives. Those who were filled with the Spirit were men of joy and peace; they were men who fellowshipped in the sufferings of Christ; they believed every word of the Old Testament; they were men of prayer. Above all, they were men with a passion for the lost. The Holy Spirit had come to give them power for one great purpose, to be witnesses for Christ to the uttermost parts of the earth (Acts 1:8). As the Father sent Christ, so He was sending these disciples.

All of this and much more is involved in the gift of God the Holy Spirit to these disciples. We read in Matthew, "How much more will your Father who is in heaven give good things to them that ask him?" (Matt. 7:11). In

Luke we read, "How much more shall your heavenly Father give the Holy Spirit to those who ask Him?" (Luke 11:13). These are not two different statements. The way God gives good things is to give us God the Holy Spirit. He takes the things of Christ and makes them real to us. Thus, the gift of the Holy Spirit is not separated from that gift of Christ as our life.

Our Lord's first statement with regard to the Holy Spirit is that He will pray or make request of the Father. The word for "pray" here is a word that means to ask for something that belongs to the intercessor: "Demand as your due." Christ is making request of the Father for something that belongs to Him; then the Father is represented as giving the Holy Spirit (v. 16). In the second mention of the Holy Spirit our Lord says, "But the Helper (Comforter), the Holy Spirit, whom the Father will send in my name" (v. 26). In the third mention, occurring in the fifteenth chapter, our Lord says, "When the Helper comes, whom I will send to you from the Father, Spirit of truth who proceeds from the Father, He will testify of Me" (15:26). Thus, we see that what the Father does the Son also does. These three representations are not contradictions, but they supplement one another. The Son makes request of the Father. The Father sends in the name of the Son. The Son Himself sends from the Father.

The question arises as to the difference between the work of the Holy Spirit when He came at Pentecost, as promised by the Lord, and the work of the Holy Spirit in the disciples before that day. The Holy Spirit is God. He was always in the world. We are told that John the Baptist was filled with the Holy Spirit from his mother's womb. All of the Old Testament saints were born of the Spirit. They did all their work by the power of the Holy Spirit. The Lord Jesus Himself worked and lived by the power of the Spirit. It was through the Holy Spirit that Peter made his great confession, and that the other saints in Gospel days were born of God.

But this new gift that the Lord is speaking of is the coming of the Holy Spirit into the hearts of believers in a new way. We are told distinctly,

"The Holy Spirit was not yet given: because Jesus was not yet glorified" (John 7:39). The great difference in the work of the Holy Spirit before and after Pentecost is the difference made by the death and resurrection of the Lord Jesus Christ. The Holy Spirit's work today is to witness to the risen, glorified Lord. This He could not do before that great event had taken place. Christ must first be glorified through death and resurrection. Then when Christ was glorified at the right hand of God, the Holy Spirit was sent to glorify Christ in the hearts of believers. Christ is all glorious; He cannot be made more glorious, but His glory is revealed. The Holy Spirit takes of the things of Christ and manifests them in and through believers. Thus does the world see Jesus living in those who are filled by the Holy Spirit.

In the sixteenth chapter, the Lord explains that when the Holy Spirit comes to the disciples He will convict the world of sin, of righteousness, of judgment. "Of sin, because they do not believe in Me; of righteousness, because I go to My Father, and you see me no more; of judgment, because the prince of this world is judged" (John 16:9-11). These are the three things that the Holy Spirit was doing through the Lord Jesus in the days of His flesh. As He walked among men, men were convicted of sin, of righteousness, of judgment. Now men can see Him no more. But men are still convicted of the sin of rejecting Jesus through the work of the Holy Spirit in individual believers, and in the Church. They are still convicted of what righteousness is by seeing Christ manifest in individual believers and in the Church, by the power of the Holy Spirit. They are still convicted that Satan is a defeated foe by seeing men over whom Satan has no power. Thus, does the Holy Spirit take the things of Christ and make them real to us.

By the power of the Holy Spirit, this new Body of Christ is created. Christ is the head. Each believer is baptized into the Body by the Holy Spirit, and each believer is indwelt by the Holy Spirit. All this and much more is involved in this gift that the Lord Jesus gave when He died and rose and ascended to the right hand of God. So important is this gift that all of the Gospel narratives move toward that great day when the gift was to be given. The Lord Jesus said, "I have a baptism to be baptized with; and how distressed I am till it is accomplished!" (Luke 12:50). It was accomplished when He sent the Holy Spirit. Now the Lord Jesus, instead of working through one human body, as in the days of His flesh, is working through all the members of His Body by the Holy Spirit.

Our Lord said to the disciples concerning the Holy Spirit, "You know him; for he dwells with you, and will be in you" (v. 17). Some take this to mean that the Holy Spirit was with the disciples while Jesus was in their midst, but that at Pentecost the Holy Spirit would come and abide within them. There is, of course, a truth in this. However, we must not press certain phrases, because words are not always used with the same significance. The word for "comforter" is "paraclete," and literally means "one called to be along side of." However, we would not gather from this that the Holy Spirit is not within Christians, but is simply along side of them. Rather the word suggests that as a companion and helper He is always by the side; so this expression is used to show that the Holy Spirit is the helper and strengthener who never leaves us. The Holy Spirit was to come in this new way at Pentecost. The Old Testament saints had the Holy Spirit, but He could not witness to them of Jesus as He did after the death and resurrection of Christ. John the Baptist and Old Testament saints were "filled with the Spirit." But these words have a different significance in the command to Christians, "Be filled with the Spirit," or live in the fullness of the Holy Spirit.

When our Lord speaks of the heavenly Father giving the Holy Spirit to them that ask Him, some would interpret this to mean that before Pentecost they might pray for the Holy Spirit, but that today Christians should not pray for the Holy Spirit, because He is living in them. But it is more likely that this expression to pray for the Holy Spirit means to pray for the results, or the blessings, or the power, that the Holy Spirit gives. It is a well-known use of language to speak of the cause for the effect, or the effect for the cause. So today, we may pray for the Holy Spirit in the sense of praying for new power or praying for the gifts that the Holy Spirit makes possible. Christians today should never ask for the Holy Spirit to come into their hearts as though He were not there. Some have suggested that at conversion, the Holy Spirit comes to the Christian, and at a later time when a full surrender is made the Holy Spirit comes to abide within. This is not in keeping with the plain and glorious teaching of all the New Testament, that the gift of the Holy Spirit is a gift that the Father gives to everyone the very instant he accepts Jesus Christ as his Saviour and Lord. All Christians are indwelt by the Holy Spirit. And all Christians have been baptized by the Holy Spirit into the Body of Christ. Not all Christians are making use of this glorious gift. Not all Christians are living in the fullness of the Spirit. Not all Christians are controlled by the Spirit. Because we possess a gift is no proof that we are necessarily making use of that gift. And none of us is making use of all that the Holy Spirit may do for us and through us. There is need continually to "pray for the Holy Spirit" in this sense.

THE THIRD GIFT

The third gift mentioned in John Fourteen is Peace. "Peace I leave with you, my peace I give to you; not as the world gives do I give to you. Let not your heart be troubled, neither let it be afraid" (v. 27).

Surely, peace is a perfect gift. It is the gift of the untroubled heart. Our Lord's first words to the assembled disciples on the day He rose from the dead, were "Peace to you" (Luke 24:36)

When Christ came, the angels proclaimed, "On earth peace, good will toward men." When Christ came, the world was free from wars. It was called "pax Romana," the peace made possible because there was one great world empire, Rome that controlled all nations. But since the Lord Jesus has come, very few years have passed with peace among all nations.

Men are asking, some sadly, and some cynically, what is the meaning of Christ's gift of peace to the earth? Did He leave the world without leaving peace? The answer is in John Fourteen. He did not leave the world without leaving peace, and His giving of peace was a perfect giving. It was not as the world gives. This is a suggestion that every gift that the world gives will leave an aching heart. Yet the gifts of the world are what men and women are striving for. Even Christians are giving most of their time and thought and strength to getting the gifts that the world has to offer. All these gifts will disappoint. They will pass away. The permanent and perfect gift is the gift of this peace, which the Lord Jesus has given His own.

There will be a yet future fulfillment of the promise of peace on earth through Christ. The nations will beat their weapons of war into instruments of peace. But that will not be till the Prince of Peace is crowned as King of Righteousness. The nations today want peace —without God's righteousness. They want prosperity without holiness. It will never be. A world that rejected God's King and nailed Him to the Cross will have no permanent peace till Christ comes again and every knee bows before Him. Nevertheless, we are to pray for peace and tranquility today in order that the Gospel may go to the uttermost part of the earth and Christ may return. Meanwhile, there is peace in the hearts in which Christ reigns.

But if He has given peace to all believers, why are there troubled hearts among Christians? The answer may be found in the fact that the fruit of the Spirit is peace, and we may not be yielded to the Spirit. The Lord Jesus has given us peace. He has given us the Holy Spirit that He might make this real to us.

Why should peace be spoken of as one of the three important gifts, when there are multiplied thousands of gifts that the Lord gives? But peace is not just like any other gift. It is a fundamental thing. The foundation of all life must be first of all peace with God through our Lord Jesus Christ The first result mentioned of the justification through the blood of Christ is that we have peace. He made peace through His blood. This is fundamental, because men were separated from God and were at war with God. The one great essential was peace. He made peace through the blood of His cross. When He said those words on Thursday night, "My peace I leave with you," the price of that peace was His precious blood. Then again there is the peace that passes all understanding. This is the foundation for all of our Christian living, and Christian service, a heart untroubled. Do we have it? The answer is, "Yes, we do have it". Our problem is not to pray that Christ should give us peace. He has already done that. We should recognize the gift, and praise God for it, and use it. How we are to do that is suggested by the next cluster of threes, the three commands.

These three gifts have already been given to every Christian; it is because we have Christ as our Life, and the Holy Spirit as our Paraclete, and the peace of God as our present heritage, that the Lord can say, "Let not your heart be troubled."

Chapter 7

The Three Commands

Up till now we have been speaking of the things that God has done for us. But there are three definite commands in John Fourteen which indicate our responsibility. If we are not entering into all of the gifts that God has for us, it is because we are not observing these commands.

THE FIRST COMMAND

The first command is, "Let not your heart be troubled" (vss. 1, 27). Perhaps we had not thought of this as a command. A troubled heart is a sinning heart. Not that it is a sin to have a sorrowful heart or a burdened heart. Paul was "sorrowing, yet always rejoicing." One may have a trusting heart in the midst of sorrows and burdens. Perhaps we do not feel guilty of having disobeyed God when we have troubled hearts. We have not thought of worry as a sin. But surely it is one of the most ungrateful of sins, when we realize that all God's love has been poured out through Christ just in order to give us peace and have our hearts untroubled.

In any case, the word, "Let not your heart be troubled" is a command. In another portion of the Word the command is given, "Be anxious for nothing" (Phil. 4:6). But one will say, "How can I keep a command like that? How can I help having a troubled heart?"

THE SECOND COMMAND

The answer is in the second command. Indeed, the two commands might be taken together as one. Nevertheless, there is a real distinction. The second command is, "you believe in God, believe also in Me." The thought is that these Jewish disciples did believe in God; they had not yet learned the meaning of believing in the Lord Jesus Christ as their God and Saviour.

Faith is the victory that overcomes the world. Faith is our key to unlock all the unsearchable riches of Christ. We are saved by grace through faith. Grace is God giving. Faith is man receiving. But we make a great mistake about faith, unless we understand that it is believing the Father's word to His child. Believing in the Lord Jesus Christ is to believe that everything He says is true, and to commit ourselves to Him. Read each of His statements in John Fourteen and ask the question, "Do I really believe that?" No man can believe these words of Christ and have a troubled heart.

When our Lord gives the command, "Let not your heart be troubled," He follows with statements that take away all reason for a troubled heart. There is a promise of heaven; there is a promise of His coming; there is the promise of the Holy Spirit. There is the satisfying of every human need in Christ. Let us not be like the Israelites of old who had the promise of entering into His rest, who had the good tidings preached to them, "But the word which they heard did not profit them, since it was not united by faith with them that heard" (Hebrews 4:2 R. V.). Then follows the word, "For we who have believed do enter that rest" (4:3). So we who have believed enter into all the riches of John Fourteen. Again, let us remember, "Believe also in me" is a command. If we do not obey it, we are sinning. A mother or father would be more grieved by a lack of trust on the part of a child than by almost any other sin. And unbelief is the root of all sin against God.

There is a faith for special needs or particular crises, for the saving of souls or healing of the body. But this faith is the resting on Jesus for the one need. So our Lord said to Martha: "Martha, Martha, you are worried and troubled about many things. But one thing is needed," (Luke 10:41, 42). The one thing was complete trust in Christ. Mary had it. Do we?

THE THIRD COMMAND

The third command mentioned in John Fourteen is one that includes all others. "If you love me, keep my commandments" (v. 15). Again, "He who has My commandments, and keeps them, it is he that loves me" (v. 21). Again, "If anyone loves Me, he will keep My word" (v. 23). Again, "He who does not love Me, does not keep My words; and the word which you hear is not Mine, but the Father's who sent me" (v. 24).

If a man says he has faith, but has not works, can that faith save him? This is the question that the practical prophet James puts to professing Christians (James 2:14). The answer is no. That kind of faith cannot save him, because it is not faith. "Faith without works is dead," just as works without faith are dead works. Christians are not saved by trying to keep God's commandments. But Christians prove they are saved by keeping the commandments of Christ.

The beloved pastor and writer, F. B. Meyer, tells of visiting one of his parishioners, a deeply devoted servant of Christ, an old man who had to rise early to have his devotions before going to his daily tasks. F. B. Meyer saw him poring over the Book, with the candle light, and the old man lifted his head and said: "I am trying to find out if I love the Lord." Quite surprised at this, the pastor waited for his explanation. He said he had read that whoever loved the Lord keeps His commandments. "So," he said, "I am searching for some of these commandments, for I do want to love the Lord, and I do want to prove it by doing His commandments and doing the things that are pleasing in His sight."

Yes, we have our responsibility. We are to walk in the light. We are to yield ourselves to God. To surrender to Christ is not optional with a Christian. If we deliberately decide that we will not surrender our lives to Christ, that is as much as to say that Jesus Christ is not our Lord, and if He is not our Lord He is not our Saviour. It is true that there are Christians who are not yielded to Christ. But such a one does not merit the name Christian. The very word "Christian" means one who does believe in Christ and expresses it by yielding to Him. The word "abide" may be spelled "o-b-e-y." It is no accident that the Greek word for believe is closely related to the word for obey. He gives the Holy Spirit to those who obey Him. Our obedience begins when we believe Him. When we obey that command to believe in the Lord Jesus, then the other command to love one another will follow.

These are the two commandments set before Christians in First John, to believe in the Lord Jesus, and to love one another. But love is the fulfilling of the law. However, love is the motive power. Love does not tell us what is right to do in all things. We need a revelation from God as to what is right to do. This revelation He has given in the commands of the Old Testament and the New, so far as those commands are addressed to us.

There is a great need of a revival of ethical standards for young Christians. Too much stress cannot be laid upon grace. We are saved by grace, apart from all works of the law. But it is possible to misuse grace. The more we understand the meaning of grace, the more will we hate sin. The more we know the blood of Christ, the more we shall be eager to know what the will of God is. The will of God is expressed in His law. So our Lord says, "I delight to do Your will, O my God, and Your law is within my heart" (Psalm 40:8; Heb. 10:7). The word "law" has many different meanings and emphases as used in Scripture. One of these meanings is that God's law is an expression of God's will; so the commandments that our Lord speaks about in John Fourteen are an expression of His will. If we find out what it means to love God with all our heart, and to love our neighbor as yourself, we are to study to know His will for Christians.

Dr. H. Clay Trumbull wrote once a notable editorial on "Love in the Old Testament, Law in the New." He would emphasize that the Old Testament is not law without love, nor is the New Testament love without law. There are more than forty definite commandments in the twelfth chapter of Romans. Some would not call these commandments; but would call them "instruction for Christians." That is a good name, "instruction for Christians." But let us remember that God's instructions are not suggestions. They are commands. We do not merit anything by keeping God's commands; we do not take one step toward heaven. Indeed, we cannot keep one command of Christ until we first accept Him as Saviour, and then we do not keep His commands perfectly, while in this body; but we are enabled to keep His commandments, not perfectly, and never by self-effort, but by the power of the Holy Spirit, and in our own measure and degree as we are controlled by the Spirit.

The Holy Spirit works through the Word of God. He does not tell us God's will as to right standards of conduct by a direct revelation in our hearts; we are to use our intelligence to study the will of God through the commandments in His Word. Then we rely on the Holy Spirit to give us that love and power to fulfill those commands.

Under grace, God's commands are God's enablings. He gives the untroubled heart, a heart set free to keep His commandments; we walk at liberty when we seek His precepts (Psa. 119:45). "I will run the course of Your commandments, for You shall enlarge my heart"(Psa. 119:32).

Chapter 8

The Three Prayers

There is mentioned in John Fourteen a mistaken prayer, or request, by a disciple, a prayer of the Lord Jesus, which we have already studied, and then His instruction for a life of prayer for Christians.

THE FIRST PRAYER

The mistaken prayer is the prayer of Philip, "Lord, show us the Father" (v. 8). Our Lord gently rebuked Philip for asking for something which He already was giving them. This is the mistake that Christians make in coming to ask for spiritual blessing. We read, "Blessed be the God and Father of our Lord Jesus Christ, who has blessed us with every spiritual blessing in the heavenly places in Christ" (Eph. 1:3). Christians yield their lives to Christ, and then they ask Him for blessing. We constantly sing, "I need Thee every hour; oh, bless me now my Saviour, I come to Thee." The words of this beautiful hymn are true words and a right prayer. But Christians miss the meaning if they keep on asking for blessing and never receive it; they keep on coming to Christ and never get there. We have learned that Christ already has given us the Holy Spirit. He has given us peace. It is wrong to keep on asking. It hinders us from enjoying the blessing when we refuse to believe that the Lord has given the blessing. Let us also sing, "I have thee this very hour; oh, guide me now, my Saviour; I trust in thee."

Some years ago, Dr. Charles G. Trumbull, of blessed memory, was having one of his after-meetings in a conference dealing with victorious Christian living. One of the Christians present rose and said, "I have been praying for victory for fifteen years. Why have I never received it?" The quiet answer was given, "Because you have kept on praying. Stop praying, and begin praising." As the people came out of that meeting, the man who had been praying for victory for fifteen years had a glowing face. With joy and confidence he told Dr. Trumbull that he had stopped praying and was praising God for the indwelling Christ, and for the victory He was giving him. We are not to ask for things that God has given us. We are to believe we have them, and to act accordingly.

THE SECOND PRAYER

The second prayer we consider is the prayer of the Lord Jesus Himself: "And I will pray to the Father, and he shall give you another Helper (Comforter)." We have already seen that in asking for the Holy Spirit, He has asked and secured for us all things. The prayer reminds us that the Lord Jesus is our great intercessor today. He is at the right hand of God interceding for us. His prayers will be answered. He made request of the Father, and the Father did send the Holy Spirit. But the Lord Jesus has not ceased to pray for us. He prayed for Peter that his faith should not fail. He prays for us. We are lifted up when we find that some Christian who is close to God is remembering us earnestly in prayer. How our hearts should rejoice in the fact that the Lord Jesus is interceding for us! He lived His earthly life by prayer. We know not how to pray as we ought, but the Holy Spirit helps our infirmity along that line; He prays in and through us. And all of this is because of that prayer of Christ to the Father that He would send the Holy Spirit. Since the Lord Jesus prays perfectly, may we enter more and more into the things that are upon the heart of Christ, that we also may pray in the Spirit.

As we think of this prayer of Christ for us, let us be reminded that we also are to pray for Christ. The Father has promised to give the nations to Him for His inheritance, in answer to His prayer (Ps. 2:8). When we pray "Your kingdom come," we are joining in prayer for the Lord Jesus that He may enter into His inheritance. We also read that "prayer also for him will be made for him continually; and daily He shall be praised" (Ps. 72:15). When we truly pray we are praying not only in the name of the Lord Jesus but for His sake, and for His sake in that we are asking the Father to give blessing to Him.

THE THIRD PRAYER

The third reference to prayer in John Fourteen gives the secret of our present prayer life, and also the secret of a life of effective service. It is connected with that amazing promise of the Lord Jesus, "he who believes in Me, the works that I do he will do also; and greater works than these he will do, because I go to My Father" (v. 12).

There is in our English versions a period at the end of verse twelve. Verse thirteen begins a new sentence, "And whatever you ask in My name, that I will do." But it seems evident that this is not the correct punctuation. These disciples are to do greater works than the Lord Jesus did in the days of His flesh. They are to do these works definitely because Christ is going to the Father. This is connected with a truth already noted, that Christ has greater power now at the right hand of God than He had in the days of His flesh. Obviously He is not speaking of greater miracles in the sense of a greater miracle than raising Lazarus, or a greater miracle than feeding the five thousand. He is speaking of the yet greater spiritual miracles. He is speaking of the fact that at Pentecost three thousand were born of the Spirit in one day, far more than are recorded as saved during the whole of His own earthly ministry.

But who is doing those greater works? Luke starts his record in Acts, "The former account I made, O Theophilus, of all that Jesus began both to do and teach, until the day in which He was taken up." In the Acts of the Apostles we have a record of what the Lord Jesus continued to do after

He was raised from the dead. Mark tells us that they went forth preaching, "the Lord working with them" (Mark 16:20). These greater miracles are miracles done by the risen Christ, and by the power of the Holy Spirit, using the disciples who are members of His Body. But what is our part in doing those greater miracles? Let us read the sentence in verses twelve and thirteen without the period: "Most assuredly, I say to you, he who believes in Me, the works that I do he will do also; and greater works than these he will do, because I go to My Father, and whatever you ask in My name, that I will do, that the Father may be glorified in the Son. If you ask anything in My name, I will do it." (vss. 12-14).

These greater works, therefore, are done by the Lord Jesus Himself. But they are done in answer to prayer. Christian service in a very real sense is Christian praying. This does not mean that we should pray without action. It does mean that our actions are governed by our prayer of faith. The Lord Jesus works in us mightily to accomplish His purpose. Our part is prayer. We are to learn this new secret of prayer, to ask in the name of the Lord Jesus. God the Father answers the prayer. But God the Son also answers prayer. He is the one who does the work, and thus the Father is glorified in the Son.

From one standpoint there is a qualification to this prayer promise. From another standpoint, there is no qualification. On one hand, we make the mistake of forgetting the qualification; on the other, we put limitations where there ought to be no limitation.

"If you abide in Me, and My words abide in you, you will ask what you desire, and it shall be done for you," is an expression of the same truth in John 15:7. When we abide in Christ, and desire only His glory, and when we study to know His will, then we are to ask what we will, and it shall be done. But notice that apart from this qualification there is no limitation. The Lord does not say, "Ask whatsoever I will." He says, "Ask whatsoever you will." What does this mean? It means that in our prayers we may know what the will of God is. The greatest hindrance to getting prayers answered on the part of consecrated Christians is that we pray with the qualification, "If it be Your will." But, one will exclaim, should we not always pray with that limitation? If we did, it would mean that we do not expect ever to have God reveal to us what His will is. Moreover, it would give no test to our faith. It would mean that we would ask for something and wait to see what God will do. If the answer does not come, we escape easily and lazily by supposing that it was not God's will. But notice the startling way in which the Lord in the New Testament puts the responsibility of unanswered prayer up to us. All things are possible with God. All things are possible to him who believes. When we say "if you can't", our Lord answers, "If you can believe, all things are possible to him who believes" (Mark 9:23). It is because of our unbelief that the prayers are not answered.

Let us use this amazing prayer promise. There are some things in which we do not, and perhaps will not, know the will of God, at least at the time we pray. But in most things we should pray until we know God's will. Then let us pray in His name, and let us thank God for the answer. To thank Him before we see the answer—this is to pray "in faith."

There is no such thing as an unanswered prayer. That is what our Lord is telling the disciples. If we ask for something that is not wise for us to have, the Lord will answer by giving a revelation of His will concerning that. But in most things we may learn what is the will of God, and then pray for that thing and believe Him for the answer.

Since the Lord Jesus is interceding for us, how can we have troubled hearts? And since He has given us prayer, every trouble may be rolled on Him. Prayer is the cure for care: "Be anxious for nothing; but in everything by prayer…" (Phil. 4:6). As Archbishop Trench sang in his beautiful sonnet on prayer:

Why, therefore, should we . . .

ever weak or heartless be,

Anxious or troubled, when with us is prayer,

And joy and strength and courage are with Thee?

Chapter 9

The Three Comings of Christ

No one would venture to speak of "three comings of Christ" unless the Lord Himself spoke in that way. We must be safeguarded against confusing any other coming with the personal return of our Lord, which is Christ's second coming. Nevertheless, in John Fourteen we do have before us three comings of Christ.

THE FIRST COMING

Christ's first coming, indeed, is not directly spoken of in the chapter. But all that is said in the chapter centers around the fact that the Lord Jesus did come in order to reveal the Father. He came forth from the Father, and He came into the world; now He is leaving the world, and going back to the Father. Had He not come the first time, we could not have spoken of the other two comings. So He did come the first time. He came to reveal the Father. He came to open the way to take us back to the bosom of the Father. And He came the first time in order to die. This is not directly mentioned in the fourteenth chapter. But everything that is said in the fourteenth chapter is in view, of the fact that He is on the way to the cross, and He does speak of the Father's commandment, and that commandment was the commandment to die on the cross for our sin.

THE SECOND COMING

But there is in John Fourteen one of the most direct and precious promises that He would come back again. The farewell message of Christ recorded in Matthew, Mark, and Luke is His prophetic message on the

Mount of Olives. He speaks there very definitely of His coming and of the end of this age. In this personal farewell message recorded in John, he says little of these great prophetic messages. The writer of John was the one to be chosen to write the Revelation. So John has to unfold more in detail the prophetic message of Christ recorded in Matthew 24, Mark 13, and in Luke 21. In the farewell message recorded in John, it is very fitting that He should speak of His second coming in terms of His personal relation to the disciples: "And if I go and prepare a place for you, I will come again and receive you to Myself; that where I am, there you may be also" (v. 3).

When our Lord said, "Let not your heart be troubled," He followed with words that should keep them from having a troubled heart; one of these words was the promise that He was coming back again to receive them unto Himself.

The second coming of Christ is not fulfilled at the death of Christians. When Christians die before Christ comes, they go to be with Christ where He is. But when the Lord Jesus returns, He comes to where the disciples are and receives them unto Himself.

In speaking of His second coming the Lord emphasizes the fact that He is coming again to take the disciples to be with Him. Now, those disciples departed and went to be with Christ long centuries ago. But they also, in their disembodied spirits, are waiting for that great day when they will come with Christ, will be reunited with their bodies, and together with the living believers will be caught up to meet the Lord. Paul in describing this, climaxes his statement with the words, "And thus we shall always be with the Lord" (1 Thess. 4:17). There is a precious suggestion here that the Lord Jesus is talking not only to these eleven disciples but to all who will believe on Him through their word, until that day when He returns again. He is including all of us when He says, "I will come again, and receive you to Myself."

The revelation of the rapture that Paul gives in Thessalonians 4:13-18 is a revelation given to him personally by the word of the Lord. It is a blessed supplement to John 14:3, according to His word in John 16:12, "I still have many things to say to you, but you cannot bear them now." Paul's teaching in Thessalonians is not the first revelation of the fact of the rapture, but of the order of the rapture.

The biography of the Christian may be expressed in those words "with the Lord." When we take Christ as our Saviour, we begin our life "with the Lord." As we go on abiding in Him—walking by faith, living in victory, it is a life lived "with the Lord." If we should die before He comes, then we depart and go to be "with Christ" (Phil. 1:23). When He comes again, we are caught up and then we are "ever with the Lord." This is the desire of Christ, that where He is there His own may be also.

At the rapture is the completion of our salvation, in "the redemption of our body" (Rom. 8:23). The dead bodies of the saints, who are now "with Christ" will be raised, reunited with their spirits. We who are alive shall be changed in a moment, and both will have resurrection bodies like our Lord's (1 Cor. 15:51-53). Then we shall be like Him, for we shall see Him as He is (1 John 3:2).

THE THIRD COMING

But our Lord in John Fourteen spoke also of another coming. He says, "I will not leave you comfortless (literally, orphans): I will come to you" (v. 18). "A little while longer and the world will see Me no more, but you will see Me. Because I live, you will live also." (v. 19). Again He says, "My Father will love him, and We will come to him and make Our home with him" (v. 23). Again, "You have heard Me say to you, 'I am going away and coming back to you'" (v. 28).

When the Holy Spirit came at Pentecost, then the Father, Son, and Spirit came to abide in the believer. Many noted theologians say that

Christ dwells in our hearts "by the Holy Spirit." But it seems evident that Christ Himself is living in our hearts, not only in the presence of the Holy Spirit, as though the Holy Spirit took His place. In the mystery of the trinity, where the Spirit is, there the Father and the Son are. It is true that the direct work of God, so to speak, is done by the Holy Spirit, who takes the things of Christ and makes them real to us. But when Paul said, "Christ lives in me," he was not speaking of this as an identical thing with the Holy Spirit dwelling in our hearts.

This is confirmed by the message in John Fourteen. The Lord definitely spoke of the fact that He would come back again personally. We know from many other Scriptures that this refers to His return in bodily form, on that great resurrection day when we shall receive our resurrection bodies, and when our redemption shall be complete. But in distinction from that He speaks of coming to the disciples in spirit. He is leaving them for a little while, but He is coming back to abide in them.

We need to remember that the Lord Jesus is God as well as man. As God, He is spirit, and thus He abides in our hearts, while at the same time He is at the right hand of God.

Paul says that "Christ in you" is "the hope of glory" (Col. 1:27). Christ's indwelling now is the guarantee of future glory. Also, present likeness to Christ is the foreshadowing of that perfect likeness to Him at His second coming.

Those who are ignorant of the Blessed Hope, or who have given up the truth that Christ will return to the earth personally, use this truth of the spiritual presence of Christ in a wrong way. In answer to the question, Will Christ come back again? they ask, When did He ever go away? We remember His own words, "for if I do not go away, the Helper will not come to you" (John 16:7). He did go away, even as He prophesied. He did send the Holy Spirit, even as He prophesied. He will come again, in personal, bodily, visible form. And He will come before the age of universal peace and righteousness. He will come to take His Church to Himself, when the Church is complete, when the Church is made ready, and when the work of the Church is finished. That work is not many things, but one thing; for there is but one Great Commission: to take the Gospel to the uttermost part of the earth (Acts 1:8). Meanwhile He is living in our hearts, for He did come at Pentecost to abide in the hearts of all believers.

In these days of war and chaos and forebodings concerning the future, can we have untroubled hearts? Since Christ's return is the Blessed Hope, the future is all bright, beyond the dark clouds. And in the present, "He will not be afraid of evil tidings; His heart is steadfast, trusting in the Lord" (Ps. 112:7).

Chapter 10

The Three Enemies

Three great enemies of the Christian are the world, the flesh, and the devil. Two of these enemies are directly mentioned in John Fourteen, and the third is there also.

THE FIRST ENEMY

Our Lord closes His farewell message to the disciples in John 16:33, with these words: "These things I have spoken to you, that in Me you may have peace. In the world you will have tribulation; but be of good cheer, I have overcome the world." He was leaving the disciples in the world, and it was natural that through this message He should speak definitely about the world.

When He promises the Holy Spirit, He tells them: "whom the world cannot receive, because it neither sees Him nor knows Him" (v. 17). Again He makes clear that He will manifest Himself to the disciples "and not to the world" (v. 22). Again, Christ contrasts His giving of peace, with the world's giving: "not as the world gives do I give to you" (v. 27). He speaks of Satan as "the prince of this world."

All through the Gospel of John, there is the contrast between the glory that is of God and the glory that is of man. Friendship with the world is enmity against Christ. His disciples are in the world, but not of the world. Later in the message, He tells them that the world would hate them. The world loves its own. The world hated Him and the world would hate his followers (John 15:18-25). The world hated Him because the world hated the Father. Doubtless John was thinking of this farewell message of the Lord when he wrote in his first letter: "Do not love the world or the things in the world. If anyone loves the world, the love of the Father is not in him. For all that is in the world—the lust of the flesh, the lust of the eyes, and the pride of life—is not of the Father but is of the world. And the world is passing away, and the lust of it; but he who does the will of God abides forever" (1 John 2:15-17).

One of the gravest dangers of the Church in all ages has been its friendship with the world. The message in John Fourteen is a clarion call to Christians to separate from the world. The way to separate from the world is to be joined to Christ. The closer we walk with Him, the more clearly will we see that the world and that all that is in the world is an enemy of grace.

Friendship with the world is spiritual adultery. Paul, speaking in the Spirit to the Corinthians, said, "For I am jealous for you with godly jealousy. For I have betrothed you to one husband, that I may present you as a chaste virgin to Christ" (2 Cor. 11:2). Then he warned them against having their minds corrupted "from the singleness of heart and the chastity that is toward Christ". In even stronger language James describes the jealousy of the Holy Spirit over those who are! Christ's when they are turned to worldliness: "Adulterers and adulteresses! Do you not know that friendship with the world is enmity with God? Or do you think that the Scripture says in vain, "The Spirit who dwells in us yearns jealously" (Jas. 4:4, 5).

THE SECOND ENEMY

The second enemy that Christ mentions directly is Satan. He calls him "the prince of this world" (v.30). He is also called "the god of this age" (2 Cor.4:4). There is the mind of Christ, and there is the mind of Satan. Satan is the personal leader of this thing called "the world." It is not merely an impersonal influence. Satan is as definitely personal as the Lord Jesus is.

He is the highest of all created beings and fell through pride. The mind of Satan is pictured in Isaiah 14:12-15, and the mind of Christ, in sharp contrast, is pictured in Philippians 2:5-10.

But listen to the good news: "He who is in you is greater than he who is in the world" (1 John 4:4). Our Lord said that the prince of the world was coming. The direct reference is to the fact that Satan's hour was coming in the death of the Lord Jesus on the cross. Christ said in Gethsemane to the chief priests and elders, "But this is your hour, and the power of darkness" (Luke 22:53).

When the Lord said, "The ruler of this world is coming," he added, "and has nothing in Me" (v. 30). When Satan tempted the Lord at the beginning of His ministry, he had nothing in Christ. The Lord was utterly sinless, and Satan could take hold of nothing. Not only so, but Satan had no claim on Christ. Some of the ancient fathers spoke of the atonement as a ransom offered to Satan, as though God owed something to Satan because of the sin of man. The Lord's Word makes clear that He does not go to the cross because of Satan. Rather He goes because the Father gave Him commandment, and because this very death would bring Satan to naught: "Now is the judgment of this world; now the ruler of this world will be cast out" (John 12:31).

The message of John Fourteen is that Satan, our arch enemy, is a defeated foe. He has nothing in Christ. Also, he has nothing in those who are in Christ, and are trusting Christ for the victory. We have already learned this truth in connection with the promise that the Holy Spirit would convict the world of judgment "because the ruler of this world is judged" (John 16:11).

THE THIRD ENEMY

But why does Satan continue to have such power with Christians? Why does the world have a grip on the Lord's people? The answer must be found in that third enemy, which is not mentioned directly but which is in mind all through the chapter. That enemy may be called the flesh, if we would complete the triad of the world, the flesh, and the devil.

We are too prone to blame all of our sins and failures on Satan or on the world. As a matter of fact, Satan would have no power over us, and the world would have no effect on us, apart from that inward enemy. These disciples to whom the Lord was speaking had failed because of their pride. They had not yet learned the meaning of turning utterly from the world because they were utterly given to the Lord. The message all through the chapter is that they should believe in the Lord. This is the secret of the untroubled heart. It is the secret also of miracles in answer to prayer. The great enemy therefore is the unbelief in the hearts of Christians. This is another way of saying, "walking after the flesh." We walk by faith, seeing Him who is invisible and have no confidence in the flesh.

Victory over the world, the flesh and the devil, is in the cross of Christ. "And those who are Christ's have crucified the flesh with its passions and desires" (Gal. 5:24). That means that we now walk after the Spirit not after the flesh (Gal. 5:22-25). We glory "in the cross of our Lord Jesus Christ, by whom the world has been crucified to me, and I to the world." (Gal. 6:14). There are two ways—the way of the cross and the way of the world. As for Satan, "they overcame him by the blood of the Lamb and by the word of their testimony" (Rev. 12:11). So let us give our testimony with Paul, "I have been crucified with Christ; it is no longer I who live, but Christ lives in me; and the life which I now live in the flesh I live by faith in the Son of God, who loved me and gave Himself for me" (Gal. 2:20).

Since our three enemies have been conquered by the Lord Jesus, there is nothing that need trouble the trusting heart.

Chapter 11

Faith, Hope, and Love

Throughout the Word of God salvation is presented as a threefold salvation. We have salvation past, salvation present, and salvation future. More accurately we might say, "salvation begun, salvation continued, salvation completed." Peter pictures it in the opening verses of his first letter: God has "begotten us again" (salvation past); we are "kept by the power of God through faith" (salvation present); we are begotten "to an inheritance incorruptible and undefiled and that does not fade away, reserved in heaven for you, who are kept by the power of God through faith for salvation ready to be revealed in the last time" (salvation future). Paul describes the conversion of the Thessalonians thus: "How you turned to God from idols (salvation begun) to serve the living and true God; (salvation continued) and to wait for his son from heaven, . . . which delivered us from the wrath to come" (salvation future).

There is one Saviour, and one salvation, and very intimately is the threefold salvation joined together. So in our Lord's message in John Fourteen, we have the threefold salvation presented, and it might be summed up in the three great words: faith, hope, and love.

Faith is linked to the cross of Christ as the beginning of our Christian life; hope looks forward to the coming of the Lord, when our salvation will be completed. Faith works through love, which determines our present living. So we read in Hebrews that having boldness to enter into the holy place by the blood of Jesus, through the new and living way, "let us draw near with a true heart in full assurance of faith, having our hearts sprinkled from an evil conscience and our bodies washed with pure water. Let us hold fast the confession of our hope without wavering, for He who promised is faithful. And let us consider one another in order to stir up love and good works" (Heb. 10:22-24). Paul again joins together these three words in speaking of "your work of faith, and labor of love, and patience of hope in our Lord Jesus Christ" (1 Thess. 1:3).

"And now abide faith, hope, love, these three; but the greatest of these is love" (1 Cor. 13:13). Love believes all things; love hopes all things. Therefore love includes faith and hope, and this is one of the senses in which we may say that it is greatest. Faith works through love, and so they cannot be separated.

There is a very general impression among Christians that faith will come to an end when we see the Lord face to face and walk by sight, and that hope will come to an end in fruition, but that love is greatest in the sense that love will abide forever. But this is not what Paul said. He wrote, "Now abides faith, hope, love." All three abide eternally.

When our Lord says, "you believe in God, believe also in Me" (v. 2), He is speaking of a trust in God which will endure through all eternity. This trust, of course, is an expression of love.

Our Lord in John Fourteen also gave the disciples the blessed hope; they were to look forward to the great day when He would come for them. But when He comes for them, and they are with Him where He is, hope does not end. Hope looks forward to the future, and there will always be new wonders of His grace unfolding before us throughout eternity.

When our redemption is complete, there is a new beginning. Then for the first time, may we grow in grace and in the knowledge of the Lord without any hindrance.

We may think of the heart of the Gospel according to John, as love. The golden text of the book is John 3:16, the great love verse of the Bible. And the heart of John Fourteen is love. The Father's love for the Son is the Father's love for us. Because He first loved, we love Him, and we love the Father (vss. 21-23). We express that love by abiding in Him and keeping

His commandments (vss. 15, 21, 24). Perfect love casts out all fear, and this is the secret of the untroubled heart.

The cure for a troubled heart: Faith, Hope, Love.

Chapter 12

The Promises and the Purpose

Our meditation on John Fourteen must not close without asking about our Lord's central purpose in all of this message. To what end does He give us the secret of an untroubled heart? Why do we have His peace that passes all understanding? Is this gift of His grace an end in itself?

One Christian who was interested in the message concerning groups of threes in John Fourteen asked if one of the groups of three would be "three promises." No, there are more than three promises in John Fourteen. There are at least fourteen promises, and if all of the promises are divided you may discover twenty-four promises. And how many purposes are mentioned in John Fourteen? May we say that there is one central purpose?

Our Lord told the disciples that when He ascended to the right hand of God, they would be able to ask Him whatsoever they would, and they would be able to do greater works than He. Now what are those greater works? What is the purpose of them? In the last verse of the fourteenth chapter, our Lord gives expression to the purpose He had in going to the cross, "that the world may know that I love the Father." Again we may discern this central purpose in observing why the Holy Spirit was sent. The Holy Spirit was to give them untroubled hearts. To what end? The answer is given very clearly in all of our Lord's revelation concerning the Spirit, and it is at the heart of what He is saying in John Fourteen. He was given that they might be witnesses unto the Lord Jesus to the uttermost part of the earth.

John Fourteen, like every other great chapter of the Bible, is a missionary message. We are to have hearts at leisure from ourselves that we might bring to others the message of the untroubled heart. But those "others" do not include only our loved ones, our friends, our neighbors, the dwellers in our city or state or nation. There are five hundred million troubled hearts who have never even heard that Christ came and died for them, and that He has sent the Holy Spirit.

To know Christ is all of life. To make Christ known is all of Christian service. So we may say that the purpose of John Fourteen is "to know Him and to make Him known."

The Lord gives us peace for our own sake, but primarily for His own glory. God is a spirit, and they that worship Him must worship Him in spirit and in truth. God is seeking such to worship Him. So the one purpose godward is that we might have communion with Him through the Lord Jesus Christ. Then having that communion, and having that peace, we are to be in this world as He was. As the Father sent Him, so He is sending the disciples.

First then comes faith; our trust in Him is the secret of the untroubled heart. Our trust in Him means to believe that He is our Shepherd. He is now meeting all our needs. A trusting heart cannot be a troubled heart.

That faith works through love. Love expresses itself in carrying out the desires of the loved one. He has left one Great Commission to the Church, not many, but one. That commission is to take the Gospel to the uttermost part of the earth. Since we know that "God so loved the world," we know that our love can have no boundaries except the boundary of His will.

But the Great Commission is not a command only. It is a prophecy. The Holy Spirit was given to empower believers to take the Gospel to the uttermost part of the earth, and so the Blessed Hope of His coming awaits the completion of that great purpose. The completion of our own salvation, the completion of our union with Christ, awaits His coming to take us to Himself. But the coming of universal peace among nations, and